for

MARK

with grateful affection

from his colleagues at

Delbarton

7 June, 1990

ROTTEN REJECTIONS

ROTTEN REJECTIONS

A LITERARY COMPANION

PUSHCART

EDITED BY ANDRÉ BERNARD
INTRODUCTION BY BILL HENDERSON

Designed by Mary Kornblum
HUDSON STUDIO
Ossining, New York

ISBN: 0–916366–57–X

INTRODUCTION

"**S**orry, NO!" My first rejection slip. It was handwritten in 1965 by Gordon "Captain Fiction" Lish, then at *Esquire,* and was in response to a story I mailed him over the transom titled "Doc Saves a Sick Whore," about a pharmacist, a whore, and a Mexican border town. I knew nothing about pharmacists, whores, or Mexican border towns. The story was awful.

Nevertheless, I found hope in that note. Gordon said he was "sorry." That probably meant he had too many manuscripts at *Esquire* and felt terrible about rejecting me. The capital "NO" and the explanation point following . . . well I chose to overlook that portion.

I wrote several more stories, all of them turned down universally, before attempting a novel. The first submission of that novel to Harper and Row's Prize Novel Contest elicited this from David Segal, editor in chief: "You have written serious fiction. The ancient and sad question is who publishes serious fiction these days." He suggested half a dozen publishers and wished me luck.

"Serious fiction!" I was overjoyed to be recognized as serious (like Melville, Faulkner, Joyce and other heroes, I figured). Again, I chose not to hear the last part of that letter, which, if I had cared to pay attention, was telling me in a nice way that my novel was unpublishable. You can't tell a 27-year old that and expect him to listen.

Years, and dozens of bland rejections later, I published the novel myself and became a publisher, one of the lower activities on the literary ladder. Now I get to send out rejections. Remembering how they sting and cripple, I try to be kind. Usually I blame Pushcart Press for being "too small" with a "limited list" for a particular manuscript. If I were young Henderson reading such a dismissal, I might infer that Pushcart was too small for my genius. Perhaps a simple NO! without the "sorry" would be more helpful for such a genius.

You will discover all sorts of rejections in André Bernard's collection of letters, in-house memos, and historical anecdotes—the first-ever such literary collection. André is a young writer with a manuscript about to make the rounds. He is also a distinguished editor now employed by one of those gigantic New York houses that eats other publishers for lunch. Plus, André has a window in his office. A sure sign of status.

André is both rejector, and soon to be rejected, perhaps. In any case, he knows what he is talking about when it comes to agony and survival.

Samuel Beckett survived: "I wouldn't touch this with a barge pole."

Harry Crews triumphed over "Burn it, son. Burn it. Fire is a great refiner."

Theodore Dreiser bested "immoral and badly written."

Tony Hillerman made it past "get rid of all that Indian stuff."

Emily Dickinson managed to ignore "Queer—the rhymes were all wrong."

And scores of other great writers did too. Evidence to follow.

I would like to honor the brave editors who admitted their mistakes and contributed letters; the publishing secretaries who clandestinely culled carbons and in-house memos from the files; and the few writers who admitted they had ever been rejected and produced the document or the memory.

On that subject, scholars beware. Some of these kiss-offs arrive from the memories of the offended and are apt to be a bit unacademic. Even the rejectors' correspondence now and then relies on memory: Pushcart's rejection of John Kennedy Toole is in my head only—and yes, I'd do it again. (Our dates are less approximate. They are the dates of rejection and/or of publication, sometimes under a different title. Some titles were never published.)

A special thanks to John White for permission to recount literary anecdotes from his *Rejection* (Addison-Wesley, 1982), an encyclopedia of all sorts of rejection; and to Jim Charlton for permission to reprint quotations from his *Writer's Quotation Book* (Pushcart, 1985), about to go into its third, revised edition, and, if I may say so, a classic. And thanks to Mary Kornblum for her beautiful design of ugly matters.

Like the previous volumes in Pushcart's Rot Series—*Rotten Reviews* and *Rotten Reviews II*—this little book is compiled for and dedicated to writers.

We hope it will leave you laughing.
And inspired to keep on writing.

BILL HENDERSON
PUBLISHER

EDITOR'S NOTE

This book was accepted by the first publisher it was shown to. It was only later that *Rotten Rejections* itself met with rejection: one industry executive refused to discuss some now-infamous misjudgments, snarling that the very idea was "disrespectful to publishers." Another opined that both Bill Henderson and I were clearly in the terminal stages of a monstrous megalomania giving us the illusion of editorial infallibility, and who the hell were we, and hadn't we ever made a mistake! In fact, this collection contains several howlers we penned during our tenures at various publishing houses, and I assure you that Henderson and I still cringe when we see those books we so confidently, so thoroughly turned away crowding the shelves in the bookstores, inching their way into their second or fifth or tenth printings.

There have been many more rejections of books and writers later to become famous than could be included here. Some examples have simply vanished together with the houses they came from; others have been as carefully entombed as a time capsule, perhaps never to see the light of day or an inquisitive researcher's eyes again. And most rejections, alas, have been of the "not right for our list" kind, that dismal refrain editors use to accompany a graceful, painless exit. (Some of you have received your share of those letters.) We have selected instead rejections that stand on their own as minor masterpieces of the genre. Of course, everyone has wisdom in hindsight, but some of these letters were destined for greatness.

Special thanks are owed to a number of writers who dusted off old files and memories to share their experiences. Among them are Jean M. Auel, J. G. Ballard, Simon Brett, Julia Child, Mary Higgins Clark, James Dickey, Peter Dickinson, Harriet Doerr, J. P. Donleavy, Harlan Ellison, Joseph Hansen, Edward Hoagland, William Kennedy, Stephen King, James Purdy, Dr. Seuss, William L. Shirer and Julian Symons.

ANDRÉ BERNARD

REJECTIONS FROM:

W. H. ALLEN CO.
AMERICAN MERCURY
THE ATLANTIC
BLACK MASK
BOBBS, MERRILL
BONI AND LIVERIGHT
JONATHAN CAPE
CENTURY MAGAZINE
CHATTO & WINDUS
COLLIERS
WILLIAM COLLINS SONS
CORNHILL MAGAZINE
DAW BOOKS
JOHN DAY
DIAL
DOUBLEDAY
DUCKWORTH
FABER & FABER
BERNARD GEIS
VICTOR GOLLANCZ
GOOD HOUSEKEEPING
GOOD WORDS
HARCOURT, BRACE
HARPER & ROW
WILLIAM HEINEMANN
HOGARTH PRESS
HOUGHTON MIFFLIN

ALFRED KNOPF
LITTLE, BROWN
J. B. LIPPINCOTT
LONGMAN GROUP
ANDREW LYTLE
MACMILLAN
MCCLURE'S
MCGRAW-HILL
METHUEN
MURRAY'S MAGAZINE
THE NATION
THE NEW YORKER
OLYMPIA PRESS
THE PARIS REVIEW
PRENTICE-HALL
PUSHCART PRESS
REDBOOK
REVUE DE PARIS
SAN FRANCISCO EXAMINER
SATURDAY EVENING POST
SCRIBNER'S
SECKER & WARBURG
THE SMART SET
VANITY FAIR

AND OTHERS

11

WE THINK THE WORLD OF YOU
J. R. ACKERLEY
1960

... not nearly dirty enough and far too English.

"THE ABILITY TO KILL"
ERIC AMBLER
1963

(We) both enjoyed (this), especially that wonderful, crooked leading character—but it's all pretty rough stuff for us, so we'll have to pass...

WINESBURG, OHIO
SHERWOOD ANDERSON
1919

... far too gloomy for us.

THE CLAN OF THE CAVE BEAR
JEAN AUEL
1980

We are very impressed with the depth and scope of your research and the quality of your prose. Nevertheless, the length presents a unique problem, for production costs are rising and the reading public are reluctant to buy expensive novels unless the author has an established reputation such as the one enjoyed by James

Michener. In any case, we don't think we could distribute enough copies to satisfy you or ourselves.

NORTHANGER ABBEY
JANE AUSTEN
1818

We are willing to return the manuscript for the same (advance) as we paid for it.

Memo from George Bernard Shaw . . .

I finished my first book seventy-six years ago. I offered it to every publisher on the English-speaking earth I had ever heard of. Their refusals were unanimous: and it did not get into print until, fifty years later, publishers would publish anything that had my name on it. . . .

I object to publishers: the one service they have done me is to teach me to do without them. They combine commercial rascality with artistic touchiness and pettishness, without being either good business men or fine judges of literature. All that is necessary in the production of a book is an author and a bookseller, without the intermediate parasite.

BLACK OXEN
GERTRUDE ATHERTON
1923

I have no hesitation in advising you to decline Mrs. Atherton's novel . . . principally for the reason that it is an apology for adultery . . . Besides this radical immorality, the novel contains many passages of pseudo-philosophy which would give offense to religious persons.

CRASH
J. G. BALLARD
1973

The author of this book is beyond psychiatric help.

More than a dozen publishers rejected a book by the poet e e cummings. So when it was finally published it had this dedication: "No Thanks to: Farrar & Rinehart, Simon & Schuster, Coward-McCann, Limited Editions, Harcourt, Brace, Random House, Equinox Press, Smith & Haas, Viking Press, Knopf, Dutton, Harper's, Scribners, Covici, Friede." Finally published . . . by whom? By e e's mother.

Memo from Oliver Herford:

Manuscript: something submitted in haste and returned at leisure.

THE DORCHESTER TALES
JOHN BARTH
1954

Barth is really smutty, delighting in filth for its own sake, and completely incapable of being funny. What the agent hopefully calls his "great good humor" is an offensive archness and facetiousness, couched in the most stilted language and in sentences most of which are seven or so lines long.

ﯔ

John Barth's stories sound like a penny-whistle out of a wind-bag full of bad odors. He may have read Boccaccio and Chaucer, but he never learned their art of storytelling.

GILES GOAT-BOY
JOHN BARTH
1966

The beginning of this intrigued me; I thought, Shades of LOLITA! Paraphernalia like this means Nabokov has been more of an influence than we'd dared hope. Alas, the beginning is entirely misleading, and what emerges is a slightly ribald science fiction novel, bawdy rather than witty . . . while I can see this being published, and even reviewed with puzzled respect, I don't think it will help a bit to clear up the mystery of what Barth is up to as a writer. Or possibly sell enough to pay its production costs.

DREAM OF FAIR-TO-MIDDLING WOMEN
SAMUEL BECKETT
1932

I wouldn't touch this with a barge-pole. Beckett's probably a clever fellow, but here he has elaborated a slavish and rather incoherent imitation of Joyce, most eccentric in language and full of disgustingly affected passages— also *indecent:* the book is damned—and you wouldn't sell the book even on its title.

MOLLOY and MALONE DIES
SAMUEL BECKETT
1951

I couldn't read either book—that is, my eye refused to sit on the page and absorb meanings, or whatever substitutes for meaning in this kind of thing . . . This doesn't make sense and it isn't funny . . . I suspect that the real fault in these novels, if I cared to read them carefully, would be simply dullness. There's no sense considering them for publication here; the bad taste of the American public does not yet coincide with the bad taste of the French avant garde.

ZULEIKA DOBSON
MAX BEERBOHM
1911

I do not think it would interest us. The author is more highly esteemed by himself than by anyone else, and has never reached any high standard in his literary work.

THE OLD WIVES' TALE
ARNOLD BENNETT
1908

... the people themselves are so deadly and monotonously dull, so devoid of aspirations or even thoughts above the yardstick standard, so depressing and even saddening in all their social relations, that they make a most fatuous assembly to find between the covers of a book.

TALES OF SOLDIERS AND CIVILIANS
AMBROSE BIERCE
1891

... uniformly horrible and revolting. Told with some power, and now and then with strokes of wonderfully vivid description, with plots ingenious in their terror and photographic in their sickening details, we must pronounce the book too brutal to be either good art or good literature. It is the triumph of realism—realism without meaning or symbolism.

THE BRIDGE OVER THE RIVER KWAI
PIERRE BOULLE
1954

A very bad book.

THE GOOD EARTH
PEARL BUCK
1931

Regret the American public is not interested in anything on China.

Memo from Michael Joseph . . .

Publishers will tell you, with their tongue in their cheek, that every manuscript which reaches their office is faithfully read, but they are not to be believed. At least fifteen out of twenty manuscripts can be summarily rejected, usually with safety. There may be a masterpiece among them, but it is a thousand to one against.

In 1911 Marcel Proust had 800 pages of what was ultimately to become the huge complex of novels called *Remembrance of Things Past* ready for publication. Where? Who would accept such an actionless, plotless sprawl of innerness revisited? He approached the house of Fasquelle and was rejected. He went to the *Nouvelle Revue Française* and was rejected again, by a very special rejecter—the celebrated André Gide. After a third publisher, Ollendorf, had refused his manuscript (with the comment that it took him thirty pages to tell how he turned over in bed), Proust decided to pay for publication himself.

Eugène Grasset published *Du Côté de chez Swann (Swann's Way)* in November 1913. Gide read it, and the following January wrote to Proust apologizing for the rejection, which he called the "gravest error of the N.R.F....one of the most burning regrets, remorses, of my life." He explained that he had considered Proust a "snob" and a "social butterfly," had only glanced at his manuscript, and had been unimpressed by what he had glimpsed. He asked pardon. Proust forgave him and the two became good friends.

THE OUTLAW OF TORN
EDGAR RICE BURROUGHS
1927

I am not sure there is any particular value in the happy ending. It seems to be more legitimate to have both De Vac and the outlaw die in the end, leaving the lady dissolved in tears, possibly on her way to become a nun . . .

Irving Stone's first book was about Van Gogh. He took it to Alfred Knopf, and "they never opened it—the package with the manuscript got home before I did." After fifteen more rejections the book, *Lust for Life*, was finally accepted and published in 1934. It has now sold about twenty-five million copies.

UNDER THE MOONS OF MARS
EDGAR RICE BURROUGHS
1912

It is not at all probable, we think, that we can make use of the story of a Virginia soldier of fortune miraculously transported to Mars . . .

OLD CREOLE DAYS
GEORGE WASHINGTON CABLE
1879

Although we can assure you that we fully appreciate your Stories both for their originality and merit we must . . . after due consideration decline their publication . . . the *times* are not particularly promising and collections of short stories almost always unsaleable. Your proposition to furnish a list of 500 subscribers is of course an inducement but not a sufficient one.

THE POSTMAN ALWAYS RINGS TWICE
JAMES M. CAIN
1934

. . . I think it is only a matter of time before you reach out into more substantial efforts that will be capable of making some real money as books.

MASTERING THE ART OF FRENCH COOKING
JULIA CHILD, SIMONE BECK, LOUISETTE BERTHOLLE
1961

What we envisage as saleable . . . is perhaps a series of small books devoted to particular portions of the meal . . . We also feel that such a series should meet a rigorous standard of simplicity and compactness, certainly less elaborate than your present volumes, which, although we are sure are foolproof, are undeniably demanding in the time and focus of the cook, who is so apt to be mother, nurse, chauffeur, and cleaner as well.

ネ

... It is a big, expensive cookbook of elaborate information and might well prove formidable to the American housewife. She might easily clip one of these recipes out of a magazine but be frightened by the book as a whole.

Memo from Stephen King:

Early in the 1970s, before my first novel (*Carrie*) was published, I sent three chapters and an outline of a science fiction novel I'd written to a publisher. Three weeks after submission, I received my material back in the SASE with a note which was both cordial and frosty. "We are not interested in science fiction which deals with negative utopias," the letter said. "They do not sell." I muttered a few words to my wife—something to the effect that George Orwell and Jonathan Swift had done quite well with negative utopias—and tossed the book in a drawer, where it stayed for eight or nine years.

THE MYSTERIOUS AFFAIR AT STYLES
AGATHA CHRISTIE
1920

It is very interesting and has several good points, but it is not quite suitable for our list.

"JOURNEY BACK TO LOVE"
MARY HIGGINS CLARK
1962

We found the heroine as boring as her husband had.

CLAUDINE IN SCHOOL
COLETTE
1900

I wouldn't be able to sell 10 copies.

THE FLYING SWANS
PADRAIC COLUM
1957

... you get almost no sensation of a story being told, for the mind of the author and that very difficult Irish way of speaking English both get in the way.

FREYE OF THE SEVEN ISLES
JOSEPH CONRAD
1911

Its overpowering gloom makes it impossible for serialization.

WHITE BUILDINGS
HART CRANE
1926

...one has to live in a mundane world... So I am afraid that we will have to pass up *White Buildings*... It is really the most perplexing kind of poetry. One reads it with a growing irritation, not at you but at himself, for the denseness of one's own intellect.

Sometimes it seems—to writers—that the number of possible rejections of a would-be book is limited only by the number of publishers. Says the *Guinness Book of World Records*, "The greatest number of publishers' rejections for a manuscript is 106 for *World Government Crusade* by Gilbert Young..."

MAGGIE: A GIRL OF THE STREETS
STEPHEN CRANE
1893

. . . too cruel for us.

UNPUBLISHED STORY COLLECTION
HARRY CREWS
1956

Burn it, son, burn it. Fire is a great refiner.

THE IPCRESS FILE
LEN DEIGHTON
1963

Not only does this bog down in the middle, but the author tends to stay too long with non-essentials. He seems to have little idea of pace, and is enchanted with his words, his tough style, and that puts me off badly . . .

YOUNG RENNY
MAZO DE LA ROCHE
1935

Mary is wooden, Malahide a caricature, (this) is a failure and will, if published, end the Whiteoak family once and for all. It will have a disastrous effect upon your public.

"SORROWS OF CHILDHOOD"
CHARLES DICKENS
1852

I am sorry, but Brutus sacrifices unborn children of his own as well as those of other people—the "Sorrows of Childhood," long in type and long a mere mysterious name, must come out. The paper really is, like the celebrated ambassadorial appointment, "too bad."

Dickens cutting his own work from Household Words

INTO THE STONE, AND OTHER POEMS
JAMES DICKEY
1959

There's a fascination about these ... yet I simply haven't the faintest idea what he's talking about most of the time. I like cryptograms very much, but you can't send a code book along with a book of poems, and I soon get impatient not knowing the answers. We're in the communications business, aren't we?

Memo from Patrick Dennis ...

Auntie Mame circulated for five years, through the halls of fifteen publishers, and finally ended up with Vanguard Press, which, as you can see, is rather deep into the alphabet.

EARLY, UNTITLED
POETRY MANUSCRIPT
EMILY DICKINSON
1862

Queer—the rhymes were all wrong.

They are quite as remarkable for defects as for beauties and are generally devoid of true poetical qualities.

Before William Saroyan (who became one of this country's most published authors) got his first acceptance he had a pile of rejection slips thirty inches high—maybe seven thousand in all.

William Saroyan rejected the 1940 Pulitzer Prize for his play *The Time of Your Life* because, he said, business had no business judging art.

WELCOME TO HARD TIMES
E. L. DOCTOROW
1960

Things improve a bit with the rebuilding of the village but then go to hell in a hack at the end. Perhaps there is a public that can take all this with a straight face but I'm not one of them.

STONES FOR IBARRA
HARRIET DOERR
1984

As it now stands, the only thing resembling a plot in this book is the slow deterioration of the husband's health ... Perhaps if the book were reconceived as order, rationalism, industry and health struggling against chaos, fate, inertia and disease, it might pull together into an integral novel of universal scope.

THE GINGER MAN
J. P. DONLEAVY
1955

... publication of *The Ginger Man* would not be a practical proposition in this country. So much of the text would have to be excised that it would almost destroy the story, and even a certain amount of rewriting would not overcome the problem ... I do not think you will find another publisher who would be willing to undertake the publication under present circumstances.

Dr. Laurence J. Peter's competence as a discover of principles was not initially recognized. When he first submitted the manuscript of
The Peter Principle: Why Things Always Go Wrong
to McGraw-Hill in 1964, the editor replied: "I can
foresee no commercial possibilities for such a book
and consequently can offer no encouragement."

Thirty publishers and thirty turndowns later,
William Morrow & Co. paid $2,500 for the manu-
script and ordered a printing of 10,000 copies. No
one expected the book to be a big hit but it sold
more than 200,000 copies in its first year, was on
the *New York Times* best-seller list through 1970
and was translated into thirty-eight languages.

THE GREAT DAYS
JOHN DOS PASSOS
1958

I am rather offended by what seems to me quite gratu-
itous passages dealing with sex acts and natural func-
tions.

A STUDY IN SCARLET
ARTHUR CONAN DOYLE
1887

Neither long enough for a serial nor short enough for a
single story.

SISTER CARRIE
THEODORE DREISER
1900

... I cannot conceive of the book arousing the interest
or inviting the attention... of the feminine readers
who control the destinies of so many novels.

ﾞﾞ

... immoral and badly written... the choice of your
characters has been unfortunate... not the best kind of
book for a young author to make his first book.

THE TITAN
THEODORE DREISER
1914

If it is too strong for Harper then it would surely be too rich for us.

ISABEL OF BAVARIA
ALEXANDRE DUMAS
1834

Stick to drama, my dear fellow. You know you are dramatic through and through.

THE SILENCE OF HISTORY
JAMES T. FARRELL
1963

Although these manuscripts are physically a mess, they are also lousy.

SANCTUARY
WILLIAM FAULKNER
1931

Good God, I can't publish this. We'd both be in jail.

As might be expected, James Joyce's writings excited some splendidly grandiose rejections. His *Dubliners* was refused by twenty-two publishers and then shot down in flames by an irate citizen. As Joyce reported it, "When at last it was printed some very kind person bought out the entire edition and had it burnt in Dublin—a new and private *auto-da-fé*." The odyssey of his *Ulysses* was even more spectacular—it was rejected, in fire, by two governments. Parts of the novel were serialized in the New York *Little Review* in 1918–20, and after rejection by a U.S. publisher the whole book was published in France in 1922 by Sylvia Beach's Shakespeare Press. Copies were sent to America and England. They were, reported Joyce, "Seized and burnt by the Custom authorities of New York and Folkestone." Not until 1933 was the U.S. ban on *Ulysses* lifted; the book was published by Random House the following year.

SARTORIS
WILLIAM FAULKNER
1929

If the book had a plot and structure, we might suggest shortening and revisions but it is so diffuse that I don't think this would be any use. My chief objection is that you don't have any story to tell.

THIS SIDE OF PARADISE
F. SCOTT FITZGERALD
1920

... the story does not seem to work up to a conclusion;—neither the hero's career nor his character are shown to be brought to any stage which justifies an ending ... It seems to us in short that the story does not culminate in anything ...

"THUMBS UP"
F. SCOTT FITZGERALD
1936

I thought it was swell but all the femmes down here said it was horrid. The thumbs, I suppose, were too much for them.

"THOUSAND AND FIRST SHIP"
F. SCOTT FITZGERALD
1936

We have pondered for a long while over this Scott Fitzgerald poem only to conclude reluctantly that we should not take it. As a poem, it has certain grave defects, including the non-permissible rhyme in the fourth stanza ...

MADAME BOVARY
GUSTAVE FLAUBERT
1856

You have buried your novel underneath a heap of details which are well done but utterly superfluous . . .

THE DIARY OF ANNE FRANK
ANNE FRANK
1952

The girl doesn't, it seems to me, have a special perception or feeling which would lift that book above the "curiosity" level.

Memo from John Gardner . . .

One should fight like the devil the temptation to think well of editors. They are all, without exception—at least some of the time—incompetent or crazy. By the nature of their profession they read too much, with the result they grow jaded and cannot recognize talent though it dances in front of their eyes.

Peyton Place, that ersatz *Desire Under the Elms,* a mish-mash of small-town sex steamy enough to tempt, you would think, all profit-minded publishers (and what other kind, you might ask, is there?), was turned down by fourteen of them. A work as different from *Peyton Place* as can be imagined, William Appleman Williams's *The Tragedy of American Diplomacy,* was rejected by more than twenty publishers before it was finally accepted. It has now been reprinted several times and is recognized as an outstanding revisionist work. *Jonathan Livingston Seagull* also flew through some twenty rejections.

"THE LONELY"
PAUL GALLICO
1937

My dear boy, what a masterpiece! How beautifully thought out! What color, what fire! It's truly magnificent writing. It's so poetic. Do take it over to *Harper's Bazaar* where they will really know how to appreciate it.

A MAN OF PROPERTY
(from THE FORSYTE SAGA)

JOHN GALSWORTHY
1906

Take your long novel down the street to my friend William Heinemann who specializes in fiction, and sit down and write a play for me—I think you'd do *that* well.

❧

This author writes to please himself rather than to please the novel reading public and accordingly his novel lacks popular qualities . . . the average reader may be pardoned if he fails to become interested in the intricate family relations involved in the opening chapters of the book . . . from beginning to end there is not one really admirable character, and it is hard to feel sympathy even for those who undergo sorrow and suffering.

❧

. . . the slight plot, the fact that all the characters are distinctly British, both seem to make it clear that the volume would not have any real sale in this country . . .

"THE SHRIEKING SKELETON"

ERLE STANLEY GARDNER
1937

The characters talk like dictionaries, the so-called plot has whiskers on it like Spanish moss hanging from a live oak in a Louisiana bayou.

"MRS GRUNDY'S ENEMIES"
GEORGE GISSING
1882

It is too painful and would not attract the kind of reader who subscribes to our publications.

THE DESCENDANT
ELLEN GLASGOW
1897

Morbid, untrue to life and untrue to American social conditions. It looks as if the author had studied New York from a winter spent at a New York hotel.

James M. Cain's novel *The Postman Always Rings Twice* stirred up something of a sensation when it was first published in 1934. It wasn't about the postal service, it was about sex. Cain explained that he had given his book its odd title because before it was accepted for publication it was rejected many times, and each day that the postman brought a letter of rejection he rang twice.

THREE WEEKS
ELINOR GLYN
1897

This is pure bosh . . . impossible sentimental gush from first to last.

THE VISITS OF ELIZABETH
ELINOR GLYN
1907

All the men, married and single, make love to her in various ways, and she comments naively on their behavior in squeezing her arms, holding her hands, kissing her, etc. . . . At the end one has the uncomfortable feeling of having been a spectator of the operation of rubbing the bloom off a girl by a lot of worldly and more or less vulgar people.

LORD OF THE FLIES
WILLIAM GOLDING
1954

It does not seem to us that you have been wholly successful in working out an admittedly promising idea.

THE WIND IN THE WILLOWS
KENNETH GRAHAME
1908

. . . the form of the story is most unexpected.

THE TIN DRUM
GÜNTER GRASS
1961

It can never be translated.

THE WHITE GODDESS
ROBERT GRAVES
1948

I have to say that it was beyond me and failed to stir
any spark of interest ... A publisher frequently publishes many books which are too good for him, i.e.
they transcend his individual taste and scholarship,
but at least he has some inkling of what the author is
aiming at and can see that there is some reasonable
ground for publication. Here it seems to me that the
interest is so obscure and so limited ... You need for
this book a publisher who is humble enough to take it
ex cathedra.

GREEK GODS AND HEROES
ROBERT GRAVES
1960

... Graves has climbed on his hobby horse and ridden
off on it. The hobby horse is anger at the Freudian and
Jungian interpretation of the myths ... (this) will
arouse controversy instead of assent.

Memo from a Chinese Economic Journal ...

We have read your manuscript with boundless delight. If we were to publish your paper, it would be impossible for us to publish any work of lower standard. And as it is unthinkable that in the next thousand years we shall see its equal, we are, to our regret, compelled to return your divine composition, and to beg you a thousand times to overlook our short sight and timidity.

THE LAST OF THE PLAINSMEN
ZANE GREY
1908

I do not see anything in this to convince me you can write either narrative or fiction.

RIDERS OF THE PURPLE SAGE
ZANE GREY
1912

It is offensive to broadminded people who do not believe that it is wise to criticize any one denomination or religious belief.

Lee Pennington has been published in more than 300 magazines—and rejected so many thousand times that in one six-month period he papered all four walls of a room with rejection slips. ("I loved getting the $8\frac{1}{2} \times 11$ rejections more than the 3×5 ones because they covered more space.") He has also filled scrapbooks with rejection slips, used them for coasters, and given rejection parties—invitations written on the backs of rejection slips.

Other suggested uses for those slips: make lampshades of them, laminate coffee tables with them, make (as did Muriel Rukeyser) wastebaskets of them. Put them on the refrigerator so you won't eat so much.

Pennington once wrote a poem about William Faulkner, sent it off, and got back a two-page single-spaced rejection, the first two sentences of which read, "This is the worst poem in the English language. You are the worst poet in the English language." He burned that rejection letter (an act he has since repented—it would have graced his scrapbook) and sent the poem to another magazine, which accepted it "with glowing praise," and chose it as its year's best poem.

"POEM"
SARA HAARDT
1923

The poem I can't take. We have 200 or 300 bales of poetry stored in Hoboken, in the old Norddeutscher-Lloyd pier. There are 300,000 poets in America.

THE WELL OF LONELINESS
RADCLYFFE HALL
1928

... we do feel (and this is the fundamental reason for our decision not to publish) that the book will be regarded as propaganda, and that inevitably the publishers of it will have to meet not only severe criticism but a chorus of fanatical abuse which, although unjustifiable, may nevertheless do them considerable damage. That consequence we are not prepared to face, and so we must decline the book ...

THE MAN EVERYBODY WAS AFRAID OF
JOSEPH HANSEN
1975

This was put together with chewing gum and paper clips.

DESPERATE REMEDIES
THOMAS HARDY
1871

... the story is ruined by the disgusting and absurd outrage which is the key to its mystery. The violation of a young lady at an evening party, and the subsequent birth of a child, is too abominable to be tolerated ...

TESS OF THE D'URBERVILLES
THOMAS HARDY
1891

... improper explicitness.

THE POOR MAN AND THE LADY
THOMAS HARDY
1868

... there crops up in parts a certain rawness of absurdity that is very displeasing, and makes it read like some clever lad's dream: the thing hangs too loosely together ... half worthy of Balzac.

CATCH-22
JOSEPH HELLER
1961

I haven't really the foggiest idea about what the man is trying to say. It is about a group of American Army officers stationed in Italy, sleeping (but not interestingly) with each others' wives and Italian prostitutes, and talking unintelligibly to one another. Apparently the author intends it to be funny—possibly even satire—but it is really not funny on any intellectual level. He has two devices, both bad, which he works constantly . . . This, as you may imagine, constitutes a continual and unmitigated bore.

৯

It is always possible that a reader who goes in for this zany-epigram stuff will think it is a work of genius, and of course he may be right. But from your long publishing experience you will know that it is less disastrous to turn down a work of genius than to turn down talented mediocrities.

THE TORRENTS OF SPRING
ERNEST HEMINGWAY
1926

It would be in extremely rotten taste, to say nothing of being horribly cruel, should we want to publish it.

There was once in Paris a society composed of playwrights who had been hissed. They met once a month on an ill-omened day, Friday, and among their members were the young Dumas, Zola, and Offenbach.

Rudyard Kipling was rejected three times for his country's highest literary honor. He was a world famous writer when Tennyson's death left the post of Great Britain's Poet Laureate vacant in 1892. Kipling was passed over and the honor was given to a relatively unknown author, Alfred Austin. When Austin died in 1913 Kipling was even more famous—in 1907 he had won the Nobel Prize for literature; again he was rejected for a less eminent writer, Robert Bridges. In 1930 the title was given to John Masefield.

It has been said that one reason for Kipling's rejections was his poem "The Widow at Windsor," which cast Victoria as a Queen whose dominions cost the lives of her soldiers.

KON-TIKI
THOR HEYERDAHL
1952

The idea of men adrift on a raft does have a certain appeal, but for the most part this is a long, solemn and tedious Pacific voyage.

THE BLESSING WAY
TONY HILLERMAN
1970

If you insist on rewriting this, get rid of all that Indian stuff.

Memo from Edward Hoagland...

There's no percentage in a publisher writing nasty letters to authors, even those whom he is rejecting; instead, the practice is likely to rebound to his disadvantage later on. Most editors, in fact, train themselves to write blandly agreeable or at least tactful letters to all the writers they must correspond with. It becomes a professional handicap for them if they do not learn this form of discipline as a part of their trade. Writers are grudge-holders, and in their solitude will nurse and magnify any grievance and pass on news of it to other writers for the next decade. Reviewers are much more likely to go haywire with spleen... I was once rejected for an advanced writing course at Harvard because X thought that reading my first novel, *Cat Man,* felt like "being thrown into a bucket of blood," though he added that I "might be published with acclaim some day."

"THE PENSION GRILLPARZER" (from THE WORLD ACCORDING TO GARP)
JOHN IRVING
1979

. . . only mildly interesting. . . it contributes nothing new to either language or form.

THE SKETCH BOOK
WASHINGTON IRVING
1819

I entreat you to believe that I feel truly obligated by your most kind intentions towards me, and that I entertain the most unfeigned respect for your most tasteful talents. My house is completely filled with workpeople at this time, and I have only an office to transact business in; and yesterday I was wholly occupied, or I should have done myself the pleasure of seeing you. If it would not suit me to engage in the publication of your present work, it is only because I do not see that scope in the nature of it which would enable me to make those satisfactory accounts between us, without which I really feel no satisfaction in engaging.

IN THE CAGE
HENRY JAMES
1898

A duller story I have never read. It wanders through a deep mire of affected writing and gets nowhere, tells no tale, stirs no emotion but weariness. The professional critics who mistake an indirect and roundabout use of words for literary art will call it an excellent piece of work; but people who have any blood in their veins will yawn and throw it down—if, indeed, they ever pick it up.

"THE SACRED FOUNT"
HENRY JAMES
1901

It is surely the n + 1st power of Jamesiness . . . It gets decidedly on one's nerves. It is like trying to make out page after page of illegible writing. The sense of effort becomes acutely exasperating. Your spine curls up, your hair-roots prickle & you want to get up and walk around the block. There is no story—oh! but none at all . . . the *subject* is something to guess, guess all the time.

POEMS
ORRICK JOHNS
1916

I have read these poems seventy or eighty times but they still fail to give me anything even remotely approaching a thrill. My private conviction is that they are very bad, but in this I may be wrong. Why not mock me and put me to fright by sending in some superb and undoubted masterpiece?

L ewis Carroll rejected rather than was rejected, pictures rather than words. He paid for initial publication of *Alice's Adventures in Wonderland* (then titled *Alice's Adventures Under Ground*) by Macmillan in 1865 but he and his illustrator, John Tenniel, were dissatisfied with the quality of the reproductions in the first printing and rejected it. (Subsequent printings pleased author, illustrator, publisher and public.) Carroll got another artist, Henry Holiday, to illustrate *The Hunting of the Snark,* published by Macmillan in 1876, but he rejected one of Holiday's pictures, a very important one. It will be remembered that the *Hunting* ends when the Baker meets the Snark, shrieks, and disappears—because the Snark is a Boojum and as everybody knows it is

POMES PENYEACH
JAMES JOYCE
1927

They belong in the bible or the family album with the portraits.

the fate of whoever meets a Boojum to "softly and suddenly vanish away." Holiday drew a picture of the Boojum as a great squat indistinct figure radiating mindless power, and very frightening indeed. Carroll rejected it because it was too good. The unimaginable had been imagined, and that shouldn't be.

In 1889 Macmillan published a juvenile version of *Alice* (which psychologists never tire of saying is not really a children's book) with twenty of the Tenniel pictures enlarged and colored, and Carroll rejected the first printing because, he said, the colors were too gaudy. The rejected books were sent to a New York publisher who re-rejected them because, he said, the colors were too dull.

A PORTRAIT OF THE ARTIST AS A YOUNG MAN
JAMES JOYCE
1916

. . . rather discursive and the point of view is not an attractive one.

❧

It is not possible to get hold of an intelligent audience in wartime.

❧

. . . a good bit of work but it won't pay.

❧

There are many *longueurs*. Passages which, though the publisher's reader may find them interesting, will be tedious to the ordinary man among the reading public. That public will call the book, as it stands at present, realistic, unprepossessing, unattractive . . . It is too discursive, formless, unrestrained, and ugly things, ugly words, are too prominent; indeed at times they seem to be shoved in one's face, on purpose, unnecessarily. The point of view will be voted "a little sordid." . . . And at the end of the book there is a complete falling to bits; the pieces of writing and the thoughts are all in pieces and they fall like damp, ineffective rockets.

ULYSSES
JAMES JOYCE
1922

We have read the chapters of Mr. Joyce's novel with great interest, and we wish we could offer to print it. But the length is an insuperable difficulty to us at present. We can get no one to help us, and at our rate of progress a book of 300 pages would take at least two years to produce . . . I have told my servants to send the MS back to you.

THE ODYSSEY: A MODERN SEQUEL
NIKOS KAZANTZAKIS
1959

... this is a very confused affair, muddling up allusions from various mythologies, religions and literatures ... I found the whole performance a bore.

Emily Dickinson had only seven of her poems published in her lifetime (now her collected words actually fill a fat volume) but her rejecter became her friend. In 1858 Thomas Wentworth Higginson of the *Atlantic Monthly* issued an appeal for fresh talent and the Belle of Amherst sent him some of her poems. He thought her a "half-cracked poetess" and advised her not to try to get anything published. But he did offer friendship and they corresponded for several years.

IRONWEED
WILLIAM KENNEDY
1983

There is much about the novel that is very good and much that I did not like. When I throw in the balance the book's unrelenting lack of commerciality, I am afraid I just have to pass.

❧

I like William Kennedy but not enough. He's a very good writer, something no one needs to tell you or him, and his characters are terrific. I cannot explain turning this down.

SEVEN STREAMS OF NEVIS
GALWAY KINNELL
1958

I doubt that it would arouse Lamont enthusiasm— more probably it would be a cause of Lamontation.

UNTITLED SUBMISSION
RUDYARD KIPLING
1889

I'm sorry, Mr. Kipling, but you just don't know how to use the English language.

A SEPARATE PEACE
JOHN KNOWLES
1958

... embarrassingly overwrought ... strikes me as much overdone, and even pretentious ... I feel rather hopeless about his having a future.

JERUSALEM
SELMA LAGERLOF
1901

An inordinately long love story, well up toward 200,000 words ... has some unwelcome episodes of illegitimacy.

LADY CHATTERLEY'S LOVER
D. H. LAWRENCE
1928

For your own good do not publish this book.

THE RAINBOW
D. H. LAWRENCE
1915

It is unpublishable as it stands because of its flagrant love passages.

What ultimately became one of the favorite children's books of all time *The Tale of Peter Rabbit*, was prenatally "courteously rejected" by the English publisher Frederick Warne and then "returned with or without thanks by at least six [other] firms," author-illustrator Beatrix Potter noted. (According to an almost certainly apocryphal story one rejecter commented that the tale "smelled like rotting carrots.") Finally she took her savings and paid for publication herself. The little book sold so well that Warne changed his mind, took over publication, and voilà! That was more than eighty years ago, and Peter Rabbit and his friends are still selling briskly.

THE SPY WHO CAME IN FROM THE COLD
JOHN LE CARRÉ
1963

You're welcome to le Carré—he hasn't got any future.

RHYMES TO BE TRADED FOR BREAD
VACHEL LINDSAY
1912

Unpoetical poems, privately printed in pretentious but poor style.

"THE LAW OF LIFE"
JACK LONDON
1900

. . . forbidding and depressing.

GENTLEMEN PREFER BLONDES
ANITA LOOS
1925

Do you realize, young woman, that you're the first American writer ever to poke fun at sex?

Memo from Julian Symons . . .

My own first book, *The Immaterial Murder Case*, was turned down in the U.S. They wrote me a first paragraph about it that was full of praise, saying it was wonderfully funny, enjoyed reading it enormously, etc. Then the second part said: afraid it's not right for us, can't publish it, shall we destroy the ms or would you like it back!

There is a story in the trade that a publisher once accepted a book and sent it to an artist for illustrations. When he had finished, the artist sent the manuscript back—and it was returned to him with a rejection slip.

MAN MEETS DOG
KONRAD LORENZ
1952

... not quite important enough to translate and set up in competition with the many dog books that bark for attention.

UNDER THE VOLCANO
MALCOLM LOWRY
1947

Flashbacks on the character's past lives and past and present thoughts and emotions (are) often tedious and unconvincing... The book is *much too long* and over elaborate for its content... The author has overreached himself and is given to eccentric word-spinning and too much stream-of-consciousness stuff.

❧

Its quality is too rare to be successful.

A RIVER RUNS THROUGH IT
NORMAN MACLEAN
1976

These stories have trees in them.

THE DEER PARK
NORMAN MAILER
1955

This will set publishing back 25 years.

THE NAKED AND THE DEAD
NORMAN MAILER
1948

All other considerations which this book presents are subsidiary to the problem posed by the profanity and obscenity of its dialogue. In my opinion it is barely publishable.

THE ASSISTANT
BERNARD MALAMUD
1957

... superficial and unconvincing ... I do not see this book as a very well told story on any level. I do not think it would have either a good critical reception or substantial sales. Cumulatively depressing.

THE LATE GEORGE APLEY
JOHN P. MARQUAND
1936

Unpublishable.

In 1969 *Steps,* a novel by Jerzy Kosinski, won the National Book Award. Six years later a freelance writer named Chuck Ross, to test the old theory that a novel by an unknown writer doesn't have a chance, typed the first twenty-one pages of *Steps* and sent them out to four publishers as the work of "Erik Demos." All four rejected the manuscript. Two years after that he typed out the whole book and sent it, again credited to Erik Demos, to more publishers, including the original publisher of the Kosinski book, Random House. Again, all rejected it with unhelpful comments—Random House used a form letter. Altogether, fourteen publishers (and thirteen literary agents) failed to recognize a book that had already been published and had won an important prize.

"A FLEA STORY"
DON MARQUIS
1927

We like it but it is over the heads of our readers.

BRUTAL AND LICENTIOUS
JOHN MASTERS
1958

Retired curry colonels writing their reminiscences of India are two a penny.

THE RAZOR'S EDGE
W. SOMERSET MAUGHAM
1944

Not desirable. I do not find the thing good of its kind and few people like that kind ... Some of the talk is clever and some of the characters interesting, but much of the long discussion of the author's philosophy of life is tedious and the author's view pessimistic and hopeless ... I do not think that the book would have a large sale here, and while I would not say that it is impossible, I think it is distasteful.

MOBY-DICK
HERMAN MELVILLE
1851

We regret to say that our united opinion is entirely against the book as we do not think it would be at all suitable for the Juvenile Market in [England.] It is very long, rather old-fashioned, and in our opinion not deserving of the reputation which it seems to enjoy.

TYPEE
HERMAN MELVILLE
1846

It is impossible that it could be true and therefore it is without real value.

PEYTON PLACE
GRACE METALIOUS
1955

Definitely too racy for us.

ESTHER WATERS
GEORGE MOORE
1894

We like the story ourselves but there are scenes in it such as a childbirth in a hospital with full accounts of labor pains etc., which would hardly go down here and it would certainly excite surprise if published by us.

Memo from Harlan Ellison . . .

One of the very few instances of rejection for reasons other than that the material was awful, was a *Playboy* bounce for one of my best stories, a piece that has won a number of awards, and of which I'm inordinately fond. The story was "Pretty Maggie Moneyeyes" and it recounted in parallel narrative the last days of two people who never meet on this side of the grave. The first was a guy who was a righteous loser. A man who had stumbled through his life like one struck repeatedly by a ball-peen hammer. The other was a woman named Maggie, an expensive call-girl who had remained tough (but not hard) in a life filled with the possibility of personal debasement and lack of self-esteem. . . .

Having sold to *Playboy* any number of times, with stories far less accomplished (in my view), I was astonished at the strength and swiftness of the rejection. Back it came from Chicago almost by return mail. The bounce note assured me this was a knockout piece of writing, but it could not *possibly* be published in *Playboy* because the male character was weaker than the female. The woman was dominant in the philosophy and action of the story, and that would seriously unsettle *Playboy*'s "young urban male readership."

> **E**dward Fitzgerald sent the manuscript of his *The Rubáiyát of Omar Khayyám* to the editor of Fraser's Magazine in 1858.
> He waited one year for a reply.
> But he heard nothing.
> He retrieved the manuscript and published it himself—to great success.

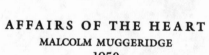

AFFAIRS OF THE HEART
MALCOLM MUGGERIDGE
1950

... the author's writing deteriorates in a peculiarly striking fashion as he lays about him with his satirical club ... a very mystifying and unsatisfactory product for the American market.

LOLITA
VLADIMIR NABOKOV
1955

It should be, and probably has been, told to a psycho-analyst, and it has been elaborated into a novel which contains some wonderful writing, but it is overwhelmingly nauseating, even to an enlightened Freudian. To the public, it will be revolting. It will not sell, and it will do immeasurable harm to a growing reputation . . . It is a totally perverse performance all around . . . the whole thing is an unsure cross between hideous reality and improbable fantasy. It often becomes a wild neurotic daydream, and the plot often gets confused, especially in the chase parts . . . It comes out as ghastly self-savagery. I am most disturbed at the thought that the writer has asked that this be published. I can see no possible cause could be served by its publication now. I recommend that it be buried under a stone for a thousand years.

PNIN
VLADIMIR NABOKOV
1957

. . . if we published it as a novel we should be blamed by the reviewers for presenting it under false pretences. And if we publish it as a collection of stories, we'd have trouble getting it read . . .

THE IMAGE AND THE LAW
HOWARD NEMEROV
1947

If the object of poetry is obscurity, Howard Nemerov is a great poet . . . I am, perhaps, a confirmed reactionary in poetry, preferring "I stood upon a little hill" and . . .

"Pepsicola hits the spot for just a nickel you get a lot" . . . Nuts, I say.

THE FOUR-CHAMBERED HEART
ANAÏS NIN
1950

Miss Nin's usual rather sensitive and lyrical writing on her usual theme of erotica interlarded with psychoanalytic interpretations . . . Miss Nin is distinctly caviar to the general public but I'm afraid it's only red caviar at that . . .

ANIMAL FARM
GEORGE ORWELL
1945

I am highly critical of many aspects of internal and external Soviet policy; but I could not possibly publish . . . a general attack of this kind.

æ

It is impossible to sell animal stories in the U.S.A.

æ

. . . highly ill-advised to publish at the present time . . . Another thing: it would be less offensive if the predominant caste in the fable were not pigs. I think the choice of pigs as the ruling caste will no doubt give offense to many people, and particularly to anyone who is a bit touchy, as undoubtedly the Russians are . . .

❧

... your pigs are far more intelligent than the other animals, and therefore the best qualified to run the farm—in fact, there couldn't have been an Animal Farm at all without them: so what was needed was not more communism but more public-spirited pigs.

DOWN AND OUT IN PARIS AND LONDON
GEORGE ORWELL
1933

It is decidedly too short...

THE SEA GOD
GEORGE ORWELL
1929

... immature and unsatisfactory... I think, too, that you deal with sex too much in your writings. Subjects a little less worldly would have a greater appeal!

THE LABYRINTH OF SOLITUDE
OCTAVIO PAZ
1962

I don't see that the whole book could be of interest to American readers. This is because it is *addressed* to Mexicans...

FOLIO CLUB TALES
EDGAR ALLAN POE
1836

Readers in this country have a decided and strong preference for works ... in which a single and connected story occupies the entire volume.

A southern writer named John Kennedy Toole wrote a comic novel about life in New Orleans called *A Confederacy of Dunces*. It was so relentlessly rejected by publishers that he killed himself. That was in 1969. His mother refused to give up on the book. She sent it out and got it back, rejected, over and over again. At last she won the patronage of Walker Percy, who got it accepted by the Louisiana State University Press, and in 1980 it won the Pulitzer Prize for fiction.

Memo from Samuel Johnson . . .

Your manuscript is both good and original; but the part that is good is not original, and the part that is original is not good.

THE CHOSEN
CHAIM POTOK
1967

. . . too long, too static, too repetitious, too ponderous and a long list of other negative "toos" . . . he has no novelistic sense whatever; he just tells you every blessed thing that the characters said and did and thought in the order in which it occurred . . . most of the time it is solidly, monumentally boring.

"PORTRAIT D'UNE FEMME"
EZRA POUND
1912

The opening line contains too many "r"s.

A DANCE TO THE MUSIC OF TIME
ANTHONY POWELL
1960

... almost too obviously Proustian in its gossipy, inconsequential detail ... a 350,000 word monstrosity that may not be any more saleable than its parts have proved.

SWANN'S WAY (REMEMBRANCE OF THINGS PAST)
MARCEL PROUST
1913

My dear fellow, I may be dead from the neck up, but rack my brains as I may I can't see why a chap should need thirty pages to describe how he turns over in bed before going to sleep.

❧

I only troubled myself so far as to open one of the notebooks of your manuscripts; I opened it at random, and, as ill luck would have it, my attention soon plunged into the cup of camomile tea on page 62—then tripped, at page 64, on the phrase ... where you speak of the "visible vertebra of a forehead."

MALCOLM
JAMES PURDY
1960

Incomprehensible.

AN UNSUITABLE ATTACHMENT
BARBARA PYM
1963

Novels like (this), despite their qualities, are getting increasingly difficult to sell.

THE SWEET DOVE DIED
BARBARA PYM
1978

Not the kind of thing to which people are turning.

In 1955 Laurence Wylie, Harvard's esteemed professor of French civilization, sent the manuscript of a sensitive chronicle of French country life, *A Village in the Vaucluse,* to Knopf. Back it came with a letter of rejection which said, "It is so far from being a book for the general reader that nothing can be done about it." Wylie did nothing "about" it—he sent it on to the Harvard University Press, which published it the next year. It became and has remained an extremely popular book for the general reader and the scholar alike.

ATLAS SHRUGGED
AYN RAND
1957

... the book is *much* too long. There are too many long speeches ... I regret to say that the book is unsaleable and unpublishable.

THE FOUNTAINHEAD
AYN RAND
1943

It is badly written and the hero is unsympathetic.

❧

This is a work of almost-genius—"genius" in the power of its expression—"almost" in the sense of its enormous bitterness. I wish there were an audience for a book of this kind. But there isn't. It won't sell.

❧

It is too intellectual for a novel.

CAPTAIN JANUARY
LAURA E. RICHARDS
1889

This is a small juvenile, written in an artificial and strained, not to say affected manner; and is neither fish, flesh nor fowl, not being suitable for children nor attractive to elders.

There is a half-baked belief among non-kitchen-minded folk that the culinary bible *Mastering the Art of French Cooking* was a much-wanted child, called into existence to satisfy a demand created by the popular TV series, *The French Chef.* Not so. *Mastering* started life as a twice-rejected orphan.

In 1953 a publisher signed a contract with Julia Child, Simone Beck, and Louisette Bertholle for a book with the working title *French Cooking for the American Kitchen.* Five years later the three cook-writers submitted their manuscript, an 850-page compendium called *French Sauces and French Poultry.* The publisher rejected it. The next year they brought back a drastically revised 684-page version titled *French Recipes for American Cooks.* The publisher rejected that too.

CASE IS CLOSED
MARY ROBERTS RINEHART
1957

I have read it, not once but twice, in an effort to find what you see in it, but I must be myopic.

ARUNDEL
KENNETH ROBERTS
1930

. . . not worth writing.

Knopf accepted it and published it in 1961 with the *Mastering* title. Though large and expensive, it sold fairly well right from the start. Impressed by the book's success, public television dreamed up the series *The French Chef,* starring Julia Child, which made its debut on February 11, 1963. That series was a smash hit from the cavalier flipping of that first-famous potato pancake onto the stove; *Mastering* mastered the air. That same year it was a Book-of-the-Month Club selection, and on November 25, 1966, Julia Child made the cover of *Time* magazine.

If the book (augmented by a second volume in 1970) were a record it would have gone platinum by now—it has sold more than a million copies.

THE TORRENT AND THE RIVER
EDWIN ARLINGTON ROBINSON
1896

We can only take refuge in the commonplace that it is next to impossible to publish successfully volumes of poems ... and we generally confine ourselves to the publication of books in whose success we can feel confidence.

VAN ZORN
EDWIN ARLINGTON ROBINSON
1914

I fancy the author of this tale reads Henry James diligently, and follows him at a *very* great distance . . . Everything is inferential, allusive, and comes to the point cautiously. The epigrams are of 'prentice-make, the humor crude, the wit invisible.

GOBLIN MARKET
CHRISTINA ROSSETTI
1862

She should exercise herself in the severest commonplace of meter until she can write as the public likes; then if she puts in her observation and passion all will become precious. But she must have Form first.

CALL IT SLEEP
HENRY ROTH
1935

As a practical commercial venture I am against it.

Memo from Joseph Hansen ...

Now and then, the media have toyed with the notion of filming my books. My encounters with media people have all been preposterous and futile, but the memory I most treasure is of a meeting in a producer's office, where he suggested the way to begin the film was to have some clod in a bar call Dave Brandstetter a "faggot," and have Dave promptly knock him down with a hard right to the jaw. The producer's secretary glanced at me, and rolled her eyes at the ceiling. In the picture business intelligence and taste are to be found only among the office help. Count on it ... It seems important to me that beginning writers ponder this—that since 1964, I have never had a book, story, or poem rejected that was not later published. If you know what you are doing, eventually you will run into an editor who knows what he/she is doing. It may take years, but never give up. Writing is a lonely business not just because you have to sit alone in a room with your machinery for hours and hours every day, month after month, year after year, but because after all the blood, sweat, toil, and tears you still have to find somebody who respects what you have written enough to leave it alone and print it. And, believe me, this remains true, whether the book is your first novel or your thirty-first.

The poet A. Wilber Stevens, later Dean of the College of Arts and Letters at the University of Nevada at Las Vegas, once sent a manuscript to the editor of a literary magazine whom he knew slightly. When his self-addressed return envelope came back to him he opened it and out fell a little pile of ashes.

CORNHUSKERS
CARL SANDBURG
1918

Good stuff, but rather out of our line. I dare you to do us a soft and luscious lyric, capable of reducing a fat woman to snuffles.

POEMS
GEORGE SANTAYANA
1922

We do not think we could sell a book of his poetry, in fact, we even fear its publication might retard his popularity.

SPECK, THE SPECIAL SARDINE
WILLIAM SAROYAN
1954

Even if Isaiah, William James, Confucius, Willa Cather and Mickey Spillane were to collaborate on an eleven-page story about a little sardine who didn't like being a sardine, and his little boy who didn't like being a little boy, I don't believe it would be a publishable book.

AND TO THINK THAT I SAW IT ON MULBERRY STREET
DR. SEUSS
1937

... too different from other juveniles on the market to warrant its selling.

THE IRRATIONAL KNOT
GEORGE BERNARD SHAW
1905

A novel of the most disagreeable kind ... the thought of the book is all wrong; the whole idea of it is odd, perverse and crude. It is the work of a man writing about life, when he knows nothing of it.

MAN AND SUPERMAN
GEORGE BERNARD SHAW
1905

... he will never be popular in the usual sense of the word, and perhaps scarcely remunerative.

AN UNSOCIAL SOCIALIST
GEORGE BERNARD SHAW
1885

... a whimsical and extravagant story, served up with a pungent literary sauce. The result is a dish, which I fancy only the few would relish.

GANDHI
WILLIAM SHIRER
1979

Too elementary.

In 1847 Charlotte Brontë (using the name Currer Bell) sent the manuscript of *The Professor* to a publishing house named Smith, Elder. That firm's letter of rejection actually encouraged the author: it discussed the book's merits and demerits "so courteously, so considerately, in a spirit so rational, with a discrimination so enlightened, that this very refusal cheered the author better than a vulgarly expressed acceptance would have done." (Later that same year Smith, Elder published *Jane Eyre*.)

> ### *Memo from Cyril Connolly:*
>
> As repressed sadists are supposed to become policemen or butchers, so those with irrational fear of life become publishers.

THE JUNGLE
UPTON SINCLAIR
1906

Sensational is a mild term for the book and the improbabilities are so glaring that even a boy reader would balk at them. It is fit only for the wastebasket.

&

I advise without hesitation and unreservedly against the publication of this book . . . it is gloom and horror unrelieved . . . One feels that what is at the bottom of his fierceness is not nearly so much desire to help the poor as hatred of the rich . . . As to the possibilities of a large sale, I should think them not very good.

IN MY FATHER'S COURT
ISAAC BASHEVIS SINGER
1966

Too pedestrian.

THE NEW MEN
C. P. SNOW
1954

It's polite, literate, plodding, sententious narrative of considerable competence but not a trace of talent or individuality; ... Real dull stuff for us Americans. The values in it are so bloody sanctimonious English that I found it hard to take.

THE MAKING OF AMERICANS
GERTRUDE STEIN
1925

We live in different worlds. Yours may hold the good, the beautiful, and the true, but if it does their guise is not for us to recognize. Those vedettes who lead the vanguard of picture arts are understood, or partly understood, over here by a reasonably compact following, but that following cannot translate their loyalties into a corresponding literature, and it would really be hopeless for us to set up this new standard.

THREE LIVES
GERTRUDE STEIN
1909

While it was conceded that there was present a literary reality—despite the foreignisms of the style—the readers felt that the strain of intensity was too unbroken and the portraits were over-complete and too infinitesimally detailed. A miniature may be overdone and apparently that is the way our readers felt about (this).

IDA: A NOVEL
GERTRUDE STEIN
1941

I am only one, only one, only. Only one being, one at the same time. Not two, not three, only one. Only one life to live, only sixty minutes in one hour. Only one pair of eyes. Only one brain. Only one being. Being only one, having only one pair of eyes, having only one time, having only one life, I cannot read your MS three or four times. Not even one time. Only one look, only one look is enough. Hardly one copy would sell here. Hardly one. Hardly one.

TRISTRAM SHANDY
LAURENCE STERNE
1759

To sport too much with your wit, or the game that wit has pointed out, is surfeiting; like toying with a man's mistress, it may be very delightful solacement to the inamorata, but little to the bystander.

A man supposedly sent a story to the *Reader's Digest* titled, "How I Made Love to a Bear." It was rejected. He rewrote it a little and retitled it "How I Made Love to a Bear in an Iron Lung" and sent it back. Again *Reader's Digest* rejected it. Another rewrite, another title change, to "How I Made Love to a Bear in an Iron Lung for the FBI," and another rejection. This time he didn't bother to rewrite at all—he just lengthened the title to "How I Made Love to a Bear in an Iron Lung for the FBI and Found God." Back came a telegram of acceptance.

LUST FOR LIFE
IRVING STONE
1934

A long, dull novel about an artist.

VALLEY OF THE DOLLS
JACQUELINE SUSANN
1966

... she is a painfully dull, inept, clumsy, undisciplined, rambling and thoroughly amateurish writer whose every sentence, paragraph and scene cries for the hand of a pro. She wastes endless pages on utter trivia, writes wide-eyed romantic scenes that would not make the back pages of *True Confessions,* hauls out every terrible show biz cliche in all the books, lets every good scene fall apart in endless talk and allows her book to ramble aimlessly ... most of the first 200 pages are virtually worthless and dreadfully dull and practically every scene is dragged out flat and stomped on by her endless talk ...

COLLECTED WORKS
J. M. SYNGE
1962

Undoubtedly they all have marked literary merit of a certain sort, but it is quite sure, it seems to me, that they would not in the slightest way appeal to the ordinary reading public of this country. For their sale you must depend on the little group of persons who are specially interested in the Irish Literary Movement or in odds and ends of pleasing literature.

"NOTUS IGNOTO"
BAYARD TAYLOR
1869

If the poem I have returned is really better than "The Sunshine of the Gods" I will eat a complete set of your works, and have dear old George Putnam thrown in for sauce. However, some day I hope to be out of this business, and quietly laid away in some uneditorial corner.

A CONFEDERACY OF DUNCES
JOHN KENNEDY TOOLE
1980

Obsessively foul and grotesque.

BARCHESTER TOWERS
ANTHONY TROLLOPE
1857

The grand defect of the work, I think, as a work of art is the low-mindedness and vulgarity of the chief actors. There is hardly a "lady" or "gentleman" among them.

"BROWN, JONES AND ROBINSON"
ANTHONY TROLLOPE
1863

You hit right and left—a wipe here, a sneer there, thrust a nasty *prong* into another place, cast a glow over Doctor Societies, a glory over balls till 4 in the morning,—in short, it is the old story—the shadow over the Church is broad and deep, and over every other quarter sunshine reigns—that is the *general impression* which the story gives, so far as it goes. There is nothing, of course, bad or vicious in it—that *could* not be, from you—but quite enough (and that without any necessity from your hand or heart) to keep [this magazine] and its Editor in boiling water until either were boiled to death.

Memo from Peter Dickinson . . .

I've been fortunate enough to have received very few rejections, and think it likely that some of my acceptances may have been a bit pig-headed. Anything by way of crass rejection would have come from my own pen or typewriter, in the days when I used to read MSS for *Punch*. I probably sent out some couple of hundred rejections a week in those days. I remember one unfortunate contributor returned to me letters I had sent him several years apart, in both of which I used the same phrase about his contribution "not quite reaching flying-speed." Hell, there's a limit to what one can say about why a piece doesn't make one laugh. We had old-fashioned roll-top desks; mine jammed once, and in the process of mending it I found a rejection-slip penned by the great editor in the early part of this century, Owen Seaman, in which he said that he thought the article most amusing but could not publish it because he did not wish to encourage drunkenness among our troops in the trenches. No date, but it must have been during the 1914–18 war.

MANKIND IN THE MAKING
H. G. WELLS
1903

. . . only a minor writer of no large promise.

THE TIME MACHINE
H. G. WELLS
1895

It is not interesting enough for the general reader and not thorough enough for the scientific reader.

THE WAR OF THE WORLDS
H. G. WELLS
1898

An endless nightmare. I do not believe it would take . . . I think the verdict would be "Oh don't read that horrid book."

THE BOOK OF MERLYN
T. H. WHITE
1950

I do wish we could get you writing again on your nature subjects.

Small, cosmetic changes can open doors. Long-mans, Green rejected a manuscript titled *The Problems of the Single Woman* only to see it become a bestseller after publication by another house as *Live Alone and Like It*. The same thing happened to a reject called *The Birds and the Bees*. It went on to prosper as *Everything You Always Wanted to Know About Sex but Were Afraid to Ask*.

LEAVES OF GRASS
WALT WHITMAN
1855

We deem it injudicious to commit ourselves.

LADY WINDERMERE'S FAN
OSCAR WILDE
1892

My dear sir,
I have read your manuscript. Oh, my dear sir.

THE PICTURE OF DORIAN GRAY
OSCAR WILDE
1891

It contains unpleasant elements.

THE DRAGON OF WONTLEY
OWEN WISTER
1892

A burlesque and grotesque piece of nonsense ... it is mere fooling and does not have the bite and lasting quality of satire.

Memo from Simon Brett ...

The only (rejection) I recall which rose above the boring was from a publisher to whom, in the late sixties or early seventies, I submitted yet another very properly unpublished novel. His reply ran: "I'm afraid the current state of the fiction market is too depressing for me to offer you any hope for this." I thought that was a very skillful rejection. While making it abundantly clear that my book had no chance at all, this situation was gracefully blamed by implication on outside factors rather than my own incompetence.

LOOK HOMEWARD, ANGEL
THOMAS WOLFE
1929

It is fearfully diffuse ... In parts, it holds one's interest by its vitality, but it is marred by stylistic clichés, outlandish adjectives and similes, etc. I do not believe it would be possible or worthwhile to doctor this up. It has all the faults of youth and inexperience.

❧

... we just can't see it. It is so long—so terribly long—that it is most difficult for a reader to sustain an interest to the end. One cannot deny that much of it has quality, if not originality—the autobiography of a young man—and so much of it has been done, and so often, that we hesitate to take another chance. We had four books of this type last year, and each one failed ... it isn't a matter of carefully editing it, or publishing it in an abridged form, it is the whole thing that must be considered. I am sorry about all this, but, having this attitude, nothing is left for us to do but decline it ...

❧

Terrible.

❧

What the manuscript lacked basically was a shape ... what was important lost its full effect because of intrusions of the commonplace.

So many books rejected by so many publishers so many times—how do those murdering bastards *feel* when they strangle yet another unborn child? William Styron's 1979 novel, *Sophie's Choice*, tells it like it was in 1947 when the hero was a forty-dollar-a-week reader for McGraw-Hill. The "lusterless drudgery" of trudging through the "club-footed syntax" and "unrelenting mediocrity" of manuscripts like *Tall Grows the Eelgrass*, by Edmonia Biersticker ("fiction ... may be the worst novel ever penned by woman or beast. Decline with all possible speed"), and *The Plumber's Wench*, by Audrey Smillie ("... absolutely imperative that this book never be published"), so stupefied the poor wretch that when a manuscript about a "long, solemn, and tedious Pacific voyage" made by "men adrift on a raft" fell into his hands he recommended rejection—"maybe a university press would buy it, but it's definitely not for us"—and the book was *Kon-Tiki*.

POEMS
WILLIAM BUTLER YEATS
1895

I am relieved to find the critics shrink from saying that Mr. Yeats will ever be a popular author. I should really

at last despair of mankind, if he could be ... absolutely
empty and void. The work does not please the ear, nor
kindle the imagination, nor hint a thought for one's re-
flection ... Do what I will, I can see no sense in the
thing: it is to me sheer nonsense. I do not say it is obscure, or uncouth or barbaric or affected—tho' it is all
these evil things; I say it is to me absolute nullity ... I
would not read a page of it again for worlds.

❧

That he has any real paying audience I find hard to believe.

Publishers say, somewhat defensively, that their
rejections are different from those of other
rejecters, not necessarily based on value judge-
ments. They may like a manuscript, they say, but
be unable to publish it because of prior commit-
ments or scheduling jams or lack of money or
other such operational obstacles. Still and all, they
have let some amazingly big fish slip through
their nets, ultimate blockbusters of all varieties:
*War and Peace, The Good Earth, The Sun Is My
Undoing, The Fountainhead, To Kill a Mockingbird,
Rubáiyát, Watership Down* ... The list goes on
and on.